RANJOT SINGH CHAHAL

Homebound Values

A Guide to Family Matters

Rana Books

First published by Rana Books (UK, India) 2023

First edition

ISBN: 978-81-19786-95-4

Contents

Chapter 1: Building Stronger Connections 1
Chapter 2: Building Trust and Mutual Respect 7
Chapter 3: Nurturing Emotional Well-being 12
Chapter 4: Fostering a Positive and Supportive Environment 19
Chapter 5: Investing in Education and Personal Growth 26
Chapter 6: Building Financial Stability and Responsibility 33
Chapter 7: Promoting Health and Well-being 38
Chapter 8: Embracing Diversity and Inclusion 46

Chapter 1: Building Stronger Connections

In today's fast-paced and digitally connected world it's easy to overlook the true value of family and family matters. However maintaining strong and healthy connections within our families is crucial for our well-being and happiness. In this chapter we will explore various aspects of building stronger connections within our families focusing on enhancing communication active listening techniques expressing appreciation and gratitude and creating meaningful moments together.

1.1 Enhancing Communication

Effective communication plays a pivotal role in fostering strong connections within families. It is not just about speaking but also about actively listening and understanding one another. Here are some key strategies for enhancing communication within your family:

Open and honest communication: Encourage family members to openly express their thoughts concerns and feelings in a safe and non-judgmental environment. This transparency helps in building trust and developing stronger bonds.

Regular family meetings: Setting aside dedicated time for family meetings can promote open dialogue and help tackle any issues or conflicts that may arise. These meetings can also serve as a platform to discuss important family matters and make decisions collectively.

Clear and respectful language: Practice using clear and respectful language when communicating with family members. Avoid blaming or criticizing and instead focus on expressing your needs and emotions in a constructive manner.

Conflict resolution: Conflicts are inevitable within any family but how we handle them defines the strength of our connections. Encourage open discussions active listening and finding common ground to resolve conflicts peacefully and promote understanding.

1.2 Active Listening Techniques

Active listening is a fundamental skill that can significantly improve communication within families. It involves giving your full attention to the speaker and seeking to understand their perspective. Here are some techniques to enhance active listening within your family:

Maintain eye contact: When someone is speaking make an effort to maintain eye contact. This demonstrates your attentiveness and shows that you value what they are saying.

Paraphrase and summarize: Repeat key points or summarize what the speaker has said to ensure you have understood their message correctly. This not only helps clarify any misunderstandings but also shows that you are genuinely interested in their perspective.

Avoid interrupting: Allow the speaker to finish their thoughts before responding. Interrupting can disrupt the flow of conversation and make the speaker feel unheard or devalued.

Show empathy: Put yourself in the speaker's shoes and try to understand their feelings and emotions. Responding with empathy fosters a deeper connection and helps build trust within the family.

Create a safe space: Encourage family members to express their thoughts and feelings without fear of judgment or criticism. When everyone feels heard and understood it strengthens the familial bond.

1.3 Expressing Appreciation and Gratitude

Expressing appreciation and gratitude towards our family members is essential in building stronger connections and fostering a positive atmosphere within the family. When we acknowledge and value each other it nurtures love respect and happiness. Here are some ways to express appreciation and gratitude within your family:

Verbal expressions: Take the time to verbally express your appreciation and gratitude towards your family members. Tell them specific reasons why you are grateful for their presence and the positive impact they have on your life.

Thank-you notes: Write heartfelt thank-you notes to your family members expressing gratitude for acts of kindness support or contribution to the family. A simple gesture like this can go a long way in strengthening familial bonds.

Acts of service: Show appreciation by performing acts of service for your family members. Help with household chores run errands or offer assistance when needed. These small acts demonstrate your willingness to support and care for your family.

Celebrating achievements: Celebrate each family member's achievements whether big or small. Recognize their efforts and express pride in their accomplishments. This positivity encourages personal growth and strengthens family bonds.

Random acts of kindness: Surprise your family members with unexpected acts of kindness. It can be as simple as preparing their favorite meal leaving encouraging notes or planning a surprise outing. These acts show thoughtfulness and affection.

1.4 Quality Time: Creating Meaningful Moments Together

In our busy lives it is easy to get caught up in everyday responsibilities and commitments leaving little time for meaningful interactions with our family members. However carving out quality time is crucial for building stronger family connections. Here are some ways to create meaningful moments together:

Family traditions: Establish and nurture family traditions that bring everyone together. It can be a weekly game night monthly family outings or annual vacations. These traditions create lasting memories and provide an opportunity for bonding.

Shared hobbies or interests: Discover and engage in activities or hobbies that the whole family can enjoy together. Whether it's cooking gardening hiking or playing sports shared interests provide a common ground for interaction and connection.

Mealtime conversations: Make mealtime a special occasion for engaging in meaningful conversations. Encourage everyone to share about their day their thoughts and interests. This creates a sense of belonging and strengthens family ties.

Technology-free zones: Designate specific times or areas in your home where technology is not allowed. This allows for uninterrupted face-to-face interactions and promotes quality time spent together.

Volunteer as a family: Engaging in community service or volunteering as a family not only helps others but also strengthens family bonds. By working together for a common cause you can instill values such as compassion empathy and teamwork.

Conclusion

Building stronger connections within our families is crucial for creating a supportive and loving environment where every member feels valued and appreciated. Enhancing communication practicing active listening expressing appreciation and gratitude and creating meaningful moments together are essential aspects of achieving this goal. By implementing these strategies and fostering a culture of love understanding and togetherness we can truly give value to family and family matters. Remember the foundation of a happy and fulfilling life can often be found within the walls of our own homes.

Chapter 2: Building Trust and Mutual Respect

2.1 Establishing Open and Honest Communication

Effective communication is the foundation for building trust and mutual respect within the family. Open and honest communication allows family members to express themselves share their thoughts and feelings and resolve conflicts in a healthy manner. When family members feel heard and understood they are more likely to trust and respect one another.

Example 1: Family Meetings

Holding regular family meetings is an excellent way to establish open and honest communication. These meetings provide a safe space for each family member to express their thoughts and concerns. During these meetings everyone should have the opportunity to speak and be heard without interruption. Topics such as upcoming events family goals or any ongoing issues can be discussed. Encouraging active listening and empathy can further promote open communication.

Example 2: Active Listening

Active listening is crucial for effective communication within the family. It involves giving your full attention to the speaker maintaining eye contact and acknowledging their feelings and perspectives. By practicing active listening family members can better understand each other's point of view and build trust. This can be particularly helpful during discussions about sensitive topics or conflicts.

2.2 Setting Boundaries and Respecting Privacy

Respecting each other's boundaries and privacy is essential for maintaining trust and mutual respect within the family. Everyone should have their own personal space and the freedom to make decisions without interference. Respecting boundaries helps create a sense of safety and autonomy fostering a positive family environment.

Example 1: Personal Space

Respecting personal space means giving each family member the freedom to have their own area where they can relax study or pursue personal interests. This could be a bedroom a designated workspace or even a corner in the living room. Encouraging family members to respect each other's personal space promotes a healthy level of independence and individuality.

Example 2: Privacy

Respecting privacy is also crucial for building trust within the family. Each family member should have the right to privacy whether it be regarding personal belongings online activities or personal conversations. Sharing passwords or accessing someone's personal belongings without permission can erode trust and lead to conflicts. Encouraging open communication about privacy needs and expectations can help establish healthy boundaries and promote trust.

2.3 Resolving Conflicts Constructively

Conflicts are a normal part of family life but how they are resolved can greatly impact the level of trust and mutual respect within the family. Handling conflicts constructively involves active listening empathy compromise and finding solutions that are beneficial to everyone involved.

Example 1: Using "I" Statements

During conflicts using "I" statements instead of blaming or accusing language can foster a more understanding and open communication environment. For example saying "I feel hurt when you interrupt me during conversations" is more effective than saying "You always interrupt me!" This approach encourages family members to express their feelings without placing blame on others making it easier to find common ground and resolve conflicts.

Example 2: Seeking Mediation

In some cases conflicts may require outside assistance to reach a resolution. Seeking mediation from a neutral third party such as a family therapist or counselor can provide a safe and structured space for family members to express their concerns and work towards finding solutions. Mediation can help rebuild broken trust and facilitate effective communication among family members.

2.4 Encouraging Individuality and Autonomy

Respecting and supporting individuality and autonomy within the family is essential for fostering trust and mutual respect. This involves recognizing and celebrating each family member's unique strengths interests and goals allowing them to express their true selves without judgment or pressure.

Example 1: Supporting Personal Interests and Goals

Encouraging and supporting each family member's personal interests and goals fosters a sense of individuality and autonomy. This can be done by actively engaging in discussions about their passions providing resources or opportunities for them to pursue their interests and celebrating their achievements. By showing interest and support family members can build trust and respect in each other's abilities and aspirations.

Example 2: Recognizing and Accepting Differences

Each family member is unique with their own set of values beliefs and perspectives. Embracing these differences and fostering an environment of acceptance allows for open and respectful communication. By appreciating diverse opinions and experiences family members can learn from one another and grow together strengthening trust and mutual respect within the family unit.

In conclusion building trust and mutual respect within the family is crucial for fostering positive relationships and a healthy family dynamic. By establishing open and honest communication setting boundaries and respecting privacy resolving conflicts constructively and encouraging individuality and autonomy families can create a supportive and nurturing environment where everyone feels valued and heard. These examples demonstrate practical ways to implement these principles and actively give value to family and family matters.

Chapter 3: Nurturing Emotional Well-being

3.1 Cultivating Emotional Intelligence

Emotional intelligence refers to the ability to recognize understand and manage our own emotions as well as recognize and empathize with the emotions of others. Nurturing emotional intelligence in the family is crucial for building strong and healthy relationships. Here are some ways to cultivate emotional intelligence within the family:

1. Encourage open communication: Create a safe and non-judgmental environment where family members feel comfortable expressing their thoughts and feelings. Encourage active listening and validate each other's emotions. This helps build empathy and understanding.

Example: When a family member is upset or angry instead of dismissing their feelings listen empathetically and try to understand their perspective. This validates their emotions and strengthens emotional bonds.

2. Teach emotional vocabulary: Help family members expand

their emotional vocabulary by introducing and discussing different emotions. This enables them to better recognize and express their own feelings and understand others' emotions.

Example: Have regular discussions about emotions during family meals or choose a "feeling of the day" to encourage family members to share their experiences and emotions.

3. Practice emotional regulation: Help family members develop healthy ways to manage their emotions such as deep breathing mindfulness or engaging in activities they enjoy. Teach them to identify triggers and develop strategies to cope effectively.

Example: When a family member is feeling overwhelmed or stressed encourage them to take a break practice mindfulness or engage in a calming activity like drawing or listening to music.

4. Model emotional intelligence: As a parent or guardian model emotional intelligence by expressing and managing your own emotions effectively. Show vulnerability and talk about how you handle difficult emotions. This teaches your family members by example.

Example: If you make a mistake acknowledge it and express your emotions honestly. This helps your family members understand that it's okay to make mistakes and express their emotions authentically.

3.2 Providing Emotional Support

Emotional support is essential for family members to feel loved accepted and understood. It involves being there for one another during both the ups and downs of life. Here are some ways to provide emotional support within the family:

1. Show empathy: Practice empathy by trying to understand and share the feelings of your family members. Validate their experiences and emotions without judgment. This helps foster a sense of connection and trust.

Example: If a family member is going through a tough time listen attentively and empathize with their emotions. Avoid dismissive comments and instead offer support and understanding.

2. Foster a culture of support: Create an environment where family members openly offer support to each other. Encourage siblings to support one another and teach them the importance of being there for family members in need.

Example: When a family member is facing a challenge encourage others to offer words of encouragement engage in problem-solving discussions or simply lend a listening ear.

3. Be present and available: Make time for your family members and be fully present when you are with them. Put away distractions and give them your undivided attention. This sends the message that you prioritize their well-being.

Example: Set aside designated quality time for family activities such as game nights outings or family dinners. During this time focus on meaningful interactions and build strong emotional connections.

4. Help problem-solve: Offer guidance and support when family members face difficulties or conflicts. Teach them effective problem-solving skills and encourage them to brainstorm solutions together.

Example: If siblings are having a disagreement mediate the situation by encouraging them to express their feelings and find common ground. Help them develop compromise and negotiation skills.

3.3 Promoting Self-Care for Every Family Member

Self-care is crucial for maintaining emotional well-being. It involves taking care of oneself physically mentally and emotionally. As a family promoting self-care can help each member thrive and feel valued. Here are some ways to promote self-care within the family:

1. Encourage healthy habits: Promote physical well-being by encouraging regular exercise a balanced diet and sufficient rest. Teach the importance of self-care practices like good hygiene and getting enough sleep.

Example: Engage in physical activities together as a family such as going for walks playing sports or doing yoga. Encourage healthy eating habits and involve children in meal planning and preparation.

2. Respect personal boundaries: Teach family members to respect each other's personal space and boundaries. Encourage open communication about individual needs for alone time and

privacy.

Example: If a family member expresses the need for alone time respect their space and give them the time they need to recharge. Encourage others to do the same.

3. Support hobbies and interests: Recognize and encourage each family member's hobbies and interests. Create opportunities for them to pursue and enjoy activities they are passionate about. This helps promote fulfillment and self-expression.

Example: If a family member enjoys painting provide them with the necessary art supplies and allocate time for them to indulge in their hobby. Show genuine interest and appreciation for their creations.

4. Teach stress management techniques: Help family members develop effective stress management techniques. Teach them mindfulness exercises deep breathing journaling or any other techniques that can help reduce stress and promote self-care.

Example: During times of stress encourage family members to take breaks practice deep breathing exercises together or engage in activities that help them relax such as reading or listening to music.

3.4 Encouraging Expressions of Love and Affection

Expressions of love and affection are vital for fostering emotional connections within the family. Encouraging genuine expressions of affection helps create a nurturing and loving environment. Here are some ways to encourage expressions of love and affection within the family:

1. Say "I love you": Encourage family members to express their love for one another verbally. Saying these simple words conveys affection and strengthens emotional bonds.

Example: Make it a habit to say "I love you" to your family members regularly both in everyday interactions and during special moments. This affirms your love for them and creates a positive emotional climate.

2. Physical affection: Encourage appropriate physical affection within the family such as hugs kisses and hand-holding. Physical touch releases feel-good hormones and promotes a sense of belonging and security.

Example: Greet family members with warm hugs and kisses offer a comforting hand on the shoulder or hold hands during walks or family outings.

3. Write love notes or letters: Encourage family members to express their love and appreciation through written words. Love notes or letters provide a lasting reminder of love and create cherished memories.

Example: Family members can write notes expressing their appreciation for each other's efforts kindness or simply letting them know they are loved. These notes can be placed in a jar or shared privately.

4. Small acts of kindness: Encourage family members to show love and affection through little gestures of kindness. These acts demonstrate care and consideration for one another.

Example: Family members can surprise each other with small gestures like making breakfast in bed leaving a thoughtful note or doing a chore for another family member without being asked.

In conclusion nurturing emotional well-being within the family is essential for building strong and healthy relationships. Cultivating emotional intelligence providing emotional support promoting self-care and encouraging expressions of love and affection contribute to a loving and supportive family environment where every member feels valued and loved. By prioritizing family matters and giving importance to emotional well-being families can develop lasting bonds and create a foundation for happiness and fulfillment.

Chapter 4: Fostering a Positive and Supportive Environment

4.1 Creating a Safe and Secure Home

Creating a safe and secure home environment is essential for nurturing strong family relationships. When family members feel safe they are more likely to open up communicate and express themselves freely. Here are some strategies to create a safe and secure home:

1. Open Communication: Encourage open and honest communication within the family. Create an atmosphere where everyone feels comfortable expressing their thoughts concerns fears and needs. This can be achieved by actively listening to each other valuing everyone's opinions and promoting empathy and understanding.

Example: Let's say there is a conflict between two siblings about sharing personal belongings. Instead of dismissing their concerns encourage them to express their feelings and talk through the issue together. This open conversation helps them feel heard and understood fostering a safe and secure environment.

2. Establish Boundaries: Set clear boundaries and rules within the family. Boundaries help create a sense of structure and predictability making everyone feel safe and secure. Make sure these boundaries align with the family's values and are communicated effectively.

Example: Establish a rule about respecting each other's privacy and personal space. This could mean that family members knock before entering someone's room or ask for permission before borrowing personal belongings. By respecting boundaries family members feel secure in their personal space.

3. Physical Safety: Ensure that the physical environment is safe for everyone in the family. Remove hazards implement safety measures and teach children about potential dangers to promote a sense of security.

Example: Install childproof locks on cabinets containing dangerous substances cover electrical outlets and secure furniture to prevent accidents. Regularly inspect the home for potential safety concerns and address them promptly.

4. Emotional Support: Provide emotional support to all family members. Create an environment where everyone feels accepted loved and valued. Encourage empathy compassion and understanding towards each other's emotions.

Example: If a family member is going through a difficult time offer a listening ear validation and support. Show empathy and try to understand their perspective offering comfort and reassurance.

4.2 Implementing Effective Discipline Techniques

Discipline is an essential aspect of family life as it helps children develop self-control responsibility and respect for others. However discipline should be implemented in a positive and constructive manner. Here are some effective discipline techniques:

1. Consistency: Establish consistent rules and consequences for behavior. When children know what is expected of them and the consequences of their actions they are more likely to make positive choices.

Example: Clearly outline rules such as completing homework before playtime or using respectful language towards each other. Consistently enforce these rules and provide appropriate consequences when they are broken such as loss of privileges or timeouts.

2. Positive Reinforcement: Focus on rewarding and reinforcing positive behavior rather than solely on punishment. Praise and acknowledge children when they exhibit desirable behavior as this motivates them to continue making positive choices.

Example: If a child consistently completes their chores without being reminded acknowledge their responsibility by offering words of praise or small rewards such as extra playtime or a special outing.

3. Natural Consequences: Allow children to experience the natural consequences of their actions whenever possible. This helps them understand the link between their behavior and the outcomes it produces.

Example: If a child forgets their lunch at home allow them to experience the consequence of going hungry for the day. This teaches them responsibility and encourages them to be more mindful in the future.

4. Time-In and Reflection: Instead of resorting to punishment or timeout use time-in as a discipline technique. This involves sitting with the child and discussing their behavior helping them reflect on their actions and learn from their mistakes.

Example: If a child exhibits aggression towards a sibling have them sit with you and calmly discuss the situation. Ask them to reflect on their behavior express their feelings and come up with alternative ways to handle conflicts.

4.3 Encouraging Positivity and Constructive Feedback

In a family fostering positivity and providing constructive feedback is crucial for the overall well-being and growth of each family member. Here are some strategies for encouraging positivity and constructive feedback:

1. Emphasize Strengths: Focus on recognizing and appreciating each family member's unique strengths and talents. Encouraging their passions and interests can boost their self-esteem and foster a positive family environment.

Example: Acknowledge and celebrate a child's artistic ability by displaying their artwork around the house attending their art shows or enrolling them in art classes to further develop their skills.

2. Practice Gratitude: Cultivate an attitude of gratitude within the family. Encourage family members to express gratitude for even the small things in life. This helps shift the focus to the positive aspects creating a more optimistic environment.

Example: Encourage each family member to share one thing they are grateful for during mealtimes or before bedtime. This simple practice promotes a positive mindset and appreciation for the good things in life.

3. Constructive Feedback: When providing feedback or addressing concerns focus on using constructive language and solutions. Avoid blaming or criticizing and instead offer guidance on how to improve or resolve issues.

Example: Instead of saying "You always make a mess!" when addressing a child's untidy room try saying "Let's work together to keep your room organized. How about setting aside some time each day to tidy up together?"

4. Encourage Support: Encourage family members to support and uplift each other. Encourage siblings to cheer each other on help with tasks and offer words of encouragement during challenging times.

Example: If a child is participating in a sports event encourage other family members to attend and show support. Celebrate the child's achievements as a family fostering a sense of unity and support.

4.4 Celebrating Achievements and Milestones

Celebrating achievements and milestones within the family provides a sense of pride accomplishment and recognition. Here are some ways to celebrate these special moments:

1. Family Celebrations: Recognize and celebrate family achievements and milestones together. This could include celebrating promotions graduations birthdays or anniversaries. Plan special activities or outings to mark these occasions and make memories together.

Example: Organize a family dinner or picnic to celebrate a child's graduation from school. Share stories express pride and shower them with words of affirmation and encouragement.

2. Personal Achievements: Acknowledge and celebrate individual achievements within the family. This could be academic achievements personal goals or personal breakthroughs. Take the time to show appreciation and recognize their efforts.

Example: If a family member has been working hard to develop a new skill such as playing a musical instrument or learning a new language celebrate their progress by hosting a small recital or congratulatory dinner.

3. Supportive Environment: Create an environment where

achievements and milestones are supported and celebrated regardless of their size or significance. Encourage family members to share their goals and aspirations and provide unwavering support.

Example: If a family member sets a personal goal such as running a marathon offer encouragement help with training and be present on race day to cheer them on. Celebrate their accomplishment and encourage them to set new goals.

4. Family Traditions: Establish family traditions around celebrating achievements and milestones. These traditions create a sense of continuity and excitement making the celebration a cherished and anticipated event.

Example: Create a tradition where each family member shares their highlight of the year during a special New Year's Eve gathering. This allows everyone to reflect on their achievements and milestones while fostering a positive and supportive environment.

In conclusion fostering a positive and supportive environment within the family is crucial for building strong relationships and promoting overall well-being. By creating a safe and secure home implementing effective discipline techniques encouraging positivity and constructive feedback and celebrating achievements and milestones families can cultivate an environment that nurtures love growth and happiness. Remember the family is a vital unit and investing time and effort into creating a positive family environment is invaluable.

Chapter 5: Investing in Education and Personal Growth

5.1 Supporting Educational Endeavors

Investing in education is one of the most important ways to give value to family and family matters. By supporting educational endeavors families empower their members to reach their full potential broaden their horizons and gain the skills and knowledge necessary for success in life.

One way to support educational endeavors is by providing financial assistance for tuition fees textbooks and other educational expenses. This can be done at any stage of education from preschool to university. For example parents can set aside a portion of their income each month for their children's education or establish educational savings accounts.

In addition to financial support families can create a conducive environment for learning at home. This includes fostering a love for reading providing a quiet study space and maintaining open lines of communication with teachers. Parents can also involve themselves in their children's educational journey by attending parent-teacher meetings volunteering at school events and engaging in regular discussions about their academic progress.

Furthermore families can emphasize the importance of education by setting high expectations and encouraging academic achievement. By making education a priority parents send a clear message to their children that learning is essential and can lead to future opportunities. They can celebrate their children's successes provide praise and encouragement and offer guidance when challenges arise.

By supporting educational endeavors families not only facilitate individual growth but also contribute to their members' overall well-being. Education opens doors to better employment opportunities promotes critical thinking and problem-solving skills and fosters personal development.

5.2 Encouraging Lifelong Learning

Beyond formal education encouraging lifelong learning is another significant way to give value to family and family matters. Lifelong learning refers to the continuous pursuit of knowledge and skills throughout one's life regardless of age or formal education. It enhances personal growth broadens perspectives and helps individuals adapt to the ever-changing world.

Families can encourage lifelong learning by fostering a culture of curiosity and intellectual exploration. This can be achieved by regularly engaging in discussions about current events encouraging reading for pleasure and exposing family members to a variety of educational resources such as documentaries podcasts and online courses.

Parents can serve as role models by demonstrating their own passion for learning. They can pursue their own interests enroll in adult education programs or engage in hobbies that stimulate intellectual engagement. By doing so they inspire their children to embrace a lifelong learning mindset.

Another way to promote lifelong learning is by encouraging family members to set personal goals and pursue new challenges. This could involve learning a new language acquiring a new skill or hobby or exploring a different field of knowledge. Families can support and motivate each other in these endeavors celebrating achievements and offering assistance when needed.

Additionally families can take advantage of community resources such as local libraries museums and educational events to provide opportunities for learning outside the home. Attending workshops lectures or cultural activities as a family can facilitate shared learning experiences and strengthen familial bonds.

By encouraging lifelong learning families demonstrate their commitment to personal growth and development. This mindset not only benefits individuals but also fosters a sense of intellectual curiosity and continuous improvement within the family unit.

5.3 Promoting Personal Development Opportunities

Investing in personal development opportunities is another way to give value to family and family matters. Personal development refers to the conscious pursuit of growth and improvement in various aspects of life including emotional well-being physical health interpersonal relationships and self-awareness.

Families can promote personal development by providing opportunities for self-reflection and self-discovery. This can be achieved through activities such as journaling mindfulness exercises and practicing gratitude. By encouraging family members to develop a deep understanding of themselves families can foster personal growth and resilience.

In addition families can support the development of life skills that are essential for success in various domains of life. These skills include communication problem-solving time management and financial literacy. By teaching and practicing these skills families empower their members to navigate challenges and achieve their goals.

Moreover families can promote emotional intelligence and mental well-being by creating a supportive and nurturing environment. This involves open and honest communication active listening empathy and understanding. Families can also seek professional help when necessary such as therapy or counseling to address and manage emotional difficulties.

Another way to promote personal development is by encouraging family members to pursue their passions and interests. Families can support each other's hobbies artistic endeavors or entrepreneurial ventures providing encouragement and celebrating achievements. This enables family members to explore their unique talents and interests fostering personal growth and fulfillment.

By promoting personal development opportunities families invest in the holistic well-being of their members. This investment not only strengthens the family unit but also equips individuals with the skills resilience and self-awareness necessary for a fulfilling and meaningful life.

5.4 Instilling Values and Moral Principles

Instilling values and moral principles is a crucial aspect of giving value to family and family matters. Values are deeply held beliefs and principles that guide individual behavior and decision-making while moral principles refer to a set of ethical standards that determine what is perceived as right or wrong.

Families play a vital role in shaping their members' values and moral compass by providing guidance modeling appropriate behavior and creating a moral framework for decision-making. This involves teaching core values such as honesty respect empathy integrity and responsibility.

Values and moral principles are imparted through consistent communication and reinforcement within the family. This can be done through family meetings discussions storytelling and role-playing scenarios to explore ethical dilemmas. By engaging in these activities families encourage critical thinking empathy and moral reasoning.

Furthermore families can expose their members to diverse cultures perspectives and experiences to foster tolerance acceptance and appreciation for differences. This can be achieved through travel participating in community service projects or engaging in intercultural interactions.

Parents and other family members serve as role models for embodying the values and moral principles they wish to instill in their family. Consistency between words and actions is essential in shaping behaviors and attitudes. By practicing what they preach parents lead by example and create a strong moral foundation for their family.

In addition to instilling values families can encourage their members to engage in ethical decision-making by providing guidance on moral reasoning. This involves discussing the consequences of choices exploring alternative perspectives and encouraging empathy and consideration for others' well-being.

By instilling values and moral principles families contribute to the development of responsible ethical and compassionate individuals. These individuals become valuable members of society making a positive difference in their communities and upholding the integrity of the family unit.

In conclusion investing in education and personal growth is crucial to give value to family and family matters. By supporting educational endeavors encouraging lifelong learning promoting personal development opportunities and instilling values and moral principles families empower their members to reach their full potential and lead fulfilling lives. These investments not only benefit individuals but also strengthen the family unit fostering resilience empathy and a sense of purpose. Investing in education and personal growth is a lifelong journey that continues to shape individuals and families for years to come.

Chapter 6: Building Financial Stability and Responsibility

6.1 Teaching Financial Literacy

Financial literacy is an essential skill that everyone should possess regardless of age or background. It involves understanding how money works including budgeting saving investing and managing debt. By teaching financial literacy to your family you can equip them with the knowledge and confidence they need to make informed financial decisions.

One way to teach financial literacy is by involving your family in discussions about money. This can include explaining basic financial concepts such as income and expenses the importance of saving and the difference between needs and wants. You can also encourage open conversations about money and answer any questions your family members may have.

Moreover you can involve your children in age-appropriate financial activities. For example you can give them an allowance and teach them how to allocate it towards different expenses such as toys or saving for a bigger purchase. You can also involve them in grocery shopping and explain the value of comparing prices and making smart purchasing decisions. By involving your family in these activities you're teaching them valuable financial skills and helping them develop a sense of responsibility.

Additionally there are various resources available to help you teach financial literacy to your family. Books online courses and interactive games can make the learning process fun and engaging for everyone involved. Make it a family activity to explore these resources together and discuss what you've learned.

6.2 Setting Financial Goals as a Family

Setting financial goals as a family is essential for building financial stability and working towards a shared vision. By setting specific measurable achievable realistic and time-bound (SMART) goals you can create a roadmap for your family's financial success.

Start by discussing your family's financial aspirations and values. For example you may prioritize saving for a down payment on a house funding your children's education or establishing an emergency fund. By identifying these goals you can align your family's financial decisions and actions with your shared vision.

Once you've identified your financial goals break them down into smaller manageable milestones. For instance if your goal is to save $50000 for a down payment in five years break it down into saving $10000 per year or $833 per month. Breaking goals into smaller achievable targets makes them more actionable and keeps everyone motivated.

Regularly review your family's progress towards your financial goals. This can be done during family meetings or through ongoing discussions. Celebrate achievements along the way and modify your plan if necessary. Remember financial goals are not set in stone and circumstances may change requiring adjustments.

By involving your family members in the goal-setting process you empower them to take ownership of their financial future. This process also strengthens family unity and cooperation as everyone works together for a common purpose.

6.3 Encouraging Budgeting and Saving

Budgeting and saving are crucial aspects of financial stability and responsibility. By encouraging these practices within your family you can instill healthy financial habits that will benefit everyone in the long run.

Start by creating a budget together as a family. Involve your children and partner in the process so that everyone has a say in how money is allocated. Begin by listing all sources of income including salaries allowances and any additional income. Then identify all necessary expenses such as housing utilities groceries and transportation. Finally allocate funds towards savings and discretionary spending.

Encourage saving by setting saving goals as a family. For example you may want to save a certain percentage of your income or work towards a specific amount for a future purchase or vacation. Make saving fun and rewarding perhaps by setting up a savings jar or using a savings app that tracks progress and provides incentives.

Teach your family the importance of distinguishing between needs and wants. Help them understand that while needs are necessities wants are desires that can be delayed or avoided. By prioritizing needs and being mindful of wants your family can make choices that align with your financial goals.

Lead by example in your own spending and saving habits. Show your family how you budget save and make smart financial decisions. Children learn from observing their parents' behaviors so being a positive financial role model can have a lasting impact.

6.4 Planning for the Future: Insurance and Estate Management

Planning for the future involves more than just budgeting and saving; it also includes protecting your family's financial well-being through insurance and estate management.

Insurance is a crucial aspect of financial stability as it provides financial protection against unexpected events. Home insurance car insurance health insurance and life insurance are examples of policies that can safeguard your family's assets and provide financial support in case of emergencies or accidents. Explain to your family the importance of having adequate insurance coverage and help them understand the different types of policies available.

Estate management refers to planning for the distribution of your assets and the care of your family in the event of your incapacity or death. It involves creating a will designating beneficiaries and possibly establishing a trust. While discussing estate planning may be uncomfortable it is essential to ensure that your family's financial affairs are taken care of in the event of unexpected circumstances. Include your family in these discussions so that they are aware of your wishes and understand the importance of estate planning.

By involving your family in these discussions and decisions you emphasize the value of family matters even when it comes to financial stability. This approach fosters open communication trust and unity within the family unit. It also serves as a reminder that financial responsibility and planning are not individual endeavors but collective efforts that contribute to the overall well-being and security of the family.

In conclusion building financial stability and responsibility within your family requires teaching financial literacy setting goals encouraging budgeting and saving and planning for the future through insurance and estate management. By involving your family in these processes and fostering open communication you create a strong foundation for financial well-being and a harmonious family dynamic.

Chapter 7: Promoting Health and Well-being

7.1 Encouraging Healthy Lifestyle Habits

Promoting healthy lifestyle habits is essential for the overall well-being of families. By instilling healthy habits families can improve their physical and mental health prevent diseases and enhance their quality of life. Let's explore some key areas of focus when it comes to encouraging healthy lifestyle habits within the family.

Firstly it is important to encourage regular physical activity. Engaging in physical activities together as a family not only promotes fitness but also enhances bonding and communication. Encouraging children to participate in sports or engaging in outdoor activities collectively helps maintain a healthy weight strengthens muscles and improves cardiovascular health. For instance going for hikes bike rides swimming or playing games like soccer or tennis can be enjoyable ways to incorporate physical activity into family routines.

Secondly limiting screen time is crucial in promoting a healthy lifestyle. Excessive use of screens such as televisions computers smartphones and tablets can lead to sedentary behavior and various health issues. It is important to establish screen time rules such as time limits and specific purposes for screen use. Encourage alternatives to screen time like reading books playing board games or engaging in creative activities. By reducing screen time families can improve their attention span sleep patterns and overall well-being.

Thirdly maintaining a balanced diet is vital for the health of every family member. Encouraging healthy eating habits and meal planning can help prevent chronic diseases and provide necessary nutrients. It is important to include a variety of fruits vegetables whole grains lean proteins and low-fat dairy products in daily meals. Engaging children in meal preparation and grocery shopping can help them develop healthier food choices. Families can also plan and cook meals together allowing for shared responsibility and reinforcing the importance of nutritious eating.

Lastly promoting regular family meals is an effective way to improve overall health and well-being. Sitting down together for meals helps foster a sense of connection and communication among family members. Research has shown that frequent family meals are associated with better academic performance improved nutrition reduced risk of obesity and eating disorders and increased emotional well-being. Encourage open and positive conversations during mealtime share experiences and make it a pleasant and relaxed environment for everyone. Make family meals a priority by scheduling them into daily routines whenever possible.

7.2 Regular Exercise and Physical Activity

Regular exercise and physical activity are essential for promoting health and well-being within families. By engaging in physical activities together families can reap numerous benefits on both physical and mental levels. Let's delve deeper into the importance of regular exercise and physical activity and explore some examples of activities families can enjoy together.

First and foremost regular exercise helps maintain a healthy weight and prevents chronic diseases such as obesity cardiovascular diseases type 2 diabetes and certain types of cancer. Engaging in physical activities that elevate heart rate and promote muscle strength and flexibility is crucial. Activities like brisk walking jogging dancing cycling swimming playing team sports and hiking are excellent ways to incorporate exercise into family routines. By participating in these activities as a family everyone can take part in the benefits of physical activity and enjoy quality time together.

Secondly regular exercise improves mental health and reduces stress and anxiety. Physical activity stimulates the release of endorphins which are natural mood boosters. Engaging in activities that challenge the body and mind such as yoga martial arts or rock climbing can provide additional benefits for both physical and mental well-being. By encouraging family members to participate in these activities together families can support each other's mental health and build stronger bonds.

Furthermore regular exercise enhances cognitive function and academic performance. Research suggests that physical activity positively impacts brain health attention span and memory. By integrating physical activity breaks into daily routines families can help children and adults stay focused and perform better in academic or work-related tasks. Engaging in activities like playing active games doing puzzles or learning a new sport can contribute to cognitive development in children and maintain mental acuity in adults.

It is important to emphasize that regular exercise and physical activity should be enjoyable and tailored to the family's preferences and abilities. By involving children and teenagers in the decision-making process families can choose activities that cater to everyone's interests and facilitate active participation. Creating a supportive and non-judgmental environment helps family members feel comfortable engaging in physical activities and motivates them to stick to a regular exercise routine.

7.3 Balanced Nutrition and Meal Planning

Balanced nutrition and meal planning play a significant role in promoting the health and well-being of families. By focusing on a nutritious and well-rounded diet families can improve their physical and mental health enhance their energy levels and reduce the risk of various diseases. Let's explore the importance of balanced nutrition and some practical tips for meal planning within the family.

Firstly balanced nutrition provides essential nutrients needed for growth development and maintenance of the body. It is important to include a variety of food groups in daily meals to ensure an adequate intake of macronutrients (carbohydrates proteins and fats) and micronutrients (vitamins and minerals). Encourage the consumption of whole grains fruits vegetables lean proteins and low-fat dairy products. Avoid excessive intake of processed foods sugary drinks and foods high in saturated fats or added sugars. By making wise choices and focusing on nutrient-dense foods families can maintain a healthy weight boost immunity and prevent chronic diseases.

Secondly involving the entire family in meal planning allows for healthier food choices and reinforces the importance of balanced nutrition. Encourage children and teenagers to participate in grocery shopping meal preparation and cooking. This involvement helps them learn about healthy food options develop cooking skills and acquire knowledge about proper portion sizes. Families can plan weekly menus together considering different preferences and dietary needs while also taking into account the nutritional value of each meal. By involving everyone in the process meals become a collaborative effort promoting family unity and creating a positive dining experience.

Furthermore meal planning helps families save time and money while promoting healthier eating habits. By planning meals in advance families can ensure they have the necessary ingredients on hand reducing the reliance on take-out or processed foods. Homemade meals tend to be healthier as they offer control over portion sizes and ingredients used. Families can also pack lunches and snacks for school or work ensuring healthier options are readily available. The act of planning and preparing meals together can be seen as a bonding activity and an opportunity to strengthen family relationships.

It is important to note that balanced nutrition does not mean strict dieting or deprivation. Families should aim for moderation and flexibility when it comes to food choices. Encouraging occasional indulgences and celebrations involving favorite foods can prevent the development of unhealthy relationships with food. By promoting a healthy and positive attitude towards eating families can create a sustainable and enjoyable approach to nutrition.

7.4 Mental Health Awareness and Support

Maintaining good mental health is fundamental for the well-being of families. By promoting mental health awareness and providing support families can better cope with challenges strengthen resilience and foster positive relationships. Let's explore the importance of mental health and some strategies for promoting well-being within the family.

Firstly it is crucial to prioritize mental health and well-being as a family. This involves open communication and creating a safe space for family members to express their thoughts and emotions without judgment. Encouraging discussions about feelings concerns and experiences helps build emotional connections and develops empathy among family members. It is essential to actively listen and validate each other's emotions offering support and understanding when needed. By fostering an emotionally supportive environment families can promote mental well-being and strengthen familial bonds.

Secondly promoting self-care practices within the family is essential for managing stress and maintaining mental health.

Encourage family members to engage in activities that bring them joy relaxation and rejuvenation. These activities can include hobbies exercise reading listening to music spending time in nature or practicing mindfulness or meditation. By prioritizing self-care and setting aside time for personal interests families can reduce stress levels improve mood and enhance overall well-being.

Additionally it is important to educate family members about mental health issues including common signs and symptoms of mental illnesses. Increasing mental health literacy within the family helps create a supportive environment and reduces stigma. Teach children and teenagers about emotions stress management and seeking help when needed. Building awareness and understanding around mental health allows families to provide appropriate support and resources when faced with challenges.

Moreover families can actively seek professional support when necessary. Mental health professionals such as therapists or counselors can provide guidance and strategies for managing mental health concerns. If a family member is experiencing significant distress or struggling with mental health issues it is important to encourage seeking professional help. By seeking therapy or counseling services families can develop coping mechanisms improve communication skills and enhance overall resilience.

In conclusion promoting health and well-being within the family is crucial for the overall happiness and satisfaction of every family member. By encouraging healthy lifestyle habits regular exercise and physical activity balanced nutrition and meal planning and mental health awareness and support families can create a foundation for optimal well-being. Engaging in physical activities together establishing screen time limits encouraging nutritious eating involving everyone in meal planning promoting open communication practicing self-care and seeking professional support when needed are essential strategies for promoting health and well-being within the family. By valuing the importance of family and focusing on their well-being families can thrive and enjoy a fulfilling life together.

Chapter 8: Embracing Diversity and Inclusion

8.1 Respecting Differences and Embracing Individuality

In today's increasingly globalized and interconnected world it is essential to respect and celebrate the differences that exist among individuals and communities. This includes embracing individuality within our own families and recognizing that each family member has unique qualities preferences and perspectives. By nurturing an environment that values diversity and encourages individuality we create a strong foundation for personal growth and healthy relationships.

Respecting differences means acknowledging that no two individuals are exactly the same and that diversity extends beyond surface-level characteristics such as race ethnicity or gender. It includes valuing differences in beliefs values interests abilities and experiences. By doing so we foster an inclusive environment where family members feel valued and accepted for who they are.

For example let's say that in a family the parents have different religious beliefs. They can create a space where they respect each other's perspectives and allow their children to explore different faiths or beliefs. By doing so they teach their children the importance of tolerance acceptance and the ability to engage in meaningful discussions and learn from others' perspectives.

Embracing individuality goes beyond merely tolerating differences; it involves celebrating them. It means recognizing and appreciating the unique abilities talents and qualities that each family member brings to the table. By doing so we encourage family members to embrace their true selves and feel empowered to pursue their passions and dreams.

For instance imagine a family where one sibling excels in sports while the other has a flair for the arts. Instead of comparing or favoring one over the other the parents can ensure both siblings receive equal support and encouragement to pursue their individual interests. This not only helps them develop their skills but also fosters a sense of self-worth and confidence.

8.2 Teaching Tolerance and Acceptance

Teaching tolerance and acceptance is crucial in promoting a harmonious and inclusive family environment. It involves instilling empathy understanding and the ability to value diverse perspectives and experiences. By teaching these fundamental values we equip our family members with the tools they need to navigate a diverse world with respect and dignity.

One effective way to teach tolerance and acceptance is through open and honest communication. Encouraging family members to express their thoughts and opinions freely while actively listening and seeking to understand helps reduce misunderstandings and promotes empathy. This nurtures an atmosphere of acceptance where everyone feels heard and valued.

For example when a family member holds a different opinion on a topic instead of dismissing their viewpoint family members can engage in meaningful conversations to understand their perspective better. This allows for the exploration of different viewpoints and encourages critical thinking while fostering tolerance and acceptance.

Another way to promote tolerance and acceptance is by exposing family members to diverse experiences and cultures. This can be done through various means such as travel participating in cultural events or engaging with individuals from different backgrounds. By exposing family members to different cultures beliefs and traditions we broaden their perspectives and foster an appreciation for diversity.

For instance a family can explore different cuisines celebrate cultural holidays from various backgrounds or engage in community activities that emphasize inclusivity. This exposure helps challenge stereotypes break down barriers and encourages a mindset of acceptance and understanding.

8.3 Cultivating Cultural Awareness and Sensitivity

Cultivating cultural awareness and sensitivity is a fundamental aspect of embracing diversity and inclusion. Cultural awareness involves recognizing and understanding the values customs and norms of different cultures. Sensitivity on the other hand refers to the ability to navigate cultural differences respectfully and effectively.

By cultivating cultural awareness and sensitivity within our families we not only promote an inclusive environment but also prepare our family members to thrive in a multicultural world. This includes fostering a sense of curiosity openness and respect towards different cultures.

To cultivate cultural awareness and sensitivity families can engage in activities that educate their members about different cultures. This could involve reading books or watching movies that highlight unique cultural experiences participating in cultural festivals or events or even inviting friends from different backgrounds to share their experiences.

For instance a family can organize a weekly "cultural exploration" session where each family member takes turns choosing a culture to explore. They can research and present various aspects like traditions food clothing and history allowing everyone to learn and appreciate the diversity that exists.

Additionally parents can encourage their children to interact with individuals from diverse backgrounds. This can be achieved through school activities community involvement or by facilitating friendships with people from different cultures. This exposure helps develop empathy reduces prejudice and builds bridges between different communities.

8.4 Supporting Social Causes and Community Involvement

Supporting social causes and actively participating in the community is another way to give value to family and demonstrate the importance of diversity and inclusion. By engaging in activities that aim to address social issues and make a positive impact we teach our family members the significance of collective action empathy and responsibility towards others.

There are numerous ways families can get involved in social causes. They can participate in volunteer programs donate to charities or organize awareness campaigns for causes they are passionate about. By working together towards a common goal families not only contribute to society but also strengthen their bonds as they collaborate for a greater purpose.

For example a family can volunteer at a local homeless shelter or food bank. By witnessing the struggles of marginalized individuals firsthand family members can develop empathy and a deeper understanding of social issues. They can also engage in discussions to brainstorm ways they can contribute effectively to address those challenges.

Moreover families can participate in events or activities that promote inclusivity and diversity within their community. This may include attending multicultural festivals supporting LGBTQ+ events or organizations or joining initiatives that promote equality and social justice. By actively involving themselves in these activities families demonstrate their commitment to embracing diversity and fostering inclusivity.

In conclusion embracing diversity and inclusion within our families is essential for personal growth healthy relationships and social progress. By respecting differences and embracing individuality teaching tolerance and acceptance cultivating cultural awareness and sensitivity and supporting social causes and community involvement we create an environment where everyone feels valued respected and empowered. By prioritizing these values within our families we can play a part in creating a more tolerant inclusive and harmonious world for future generations.

9 788119 786954

Printed at Repro India Ltd.